HELPING CHILDREN TO
BUILD SELF-CONFIDENCE

Also part of the Helping Children to Build Wellbeing and Resilience series

Helping Children to Manage Anger
Photocopiable Activity Booklet to Support Wellbeing and Resilience
Deborah M. Plummer
Illustrated by Alice Harper
ISBN 978 1 78775 863 6
eISBN 978 1 78775 864 3

Helping Children to Manage Transitions
Photocopiable Activity Booklet to Support Wellbeing and Resilience
Deborah M. Plummer
Illustrated by Alice Harper
ISBN 978 1 78775 861 2
eISBN 978 1 78775 862 9

Helping Children to Manage Stress
Photocopiable Activity Booklet to Support Wellbeing and Resilience
Deborah M. Plummer
Illustrated by Alice Harper
ISBN 978 1 78775 865 0
eISBN 978 1 78775 866 7

Using Imagination, Mindful Play and Creative Thinking to Support Wellbeing and Resilience in Children
Deborah M. Plummer
Illustrated by Alice Harper
eISBN 978 1 78775 867 4

Helping Children to Manage Friendships
Photocopiable Activity Booklet to Support Wellbeing and Resilience
Deborah M. Plummer
Illustrated by Alice Harper
ISBN 978 1 78775 868 1
eISBN 978 1 78775 869 8

Helping Children to Build Communication Skills
Photocopiable Activity Booklet to Support Wellbeing and Resilience
Deborah M. Plummer
Illustrated by Alice Harper
ISBN 978 1 78775 870 4
eISBN 978 1 78775 871 1

Helping Children *to* Build Self-Confidence

Photocopiable Activity Booklet to Support
Wellbeing and Resilience

Illustrations by Alice Harper

Jessica Kingsley Publishers
London and Philadelphia

First published in Great Britain in 2022 by Jessica Kingsley Publishers
An imprint of Hodder & Stoughton Ltd
An Hachette Company

Some material was first published in *Self-Esteem Games for Children*
[2006], *Helping Children to Build Self-Esteem* [2007], *Focusing and
Calming Games for Children* [2012], *Helping Adolescents and Adults
to Build Self-Esteem* [2014], *Inspiring and Creative Ideas for Working
with Children* [2016]. This edition first published in Great Britain
in 2022 by Jessica Kingsley Publishers.

1

A CIP catalogue record for this title is available from the
British Library and the Library of Congress

ISBN 978 1 78775 872 8
eISBN 978 1 78775 873 5

Printed and bound in Great Britain by Bell & Bain Limited

Jessica Kingsley Publishers' policy is to use papers that are natural,
renewable and recyclable products and made from wood grown
in sustainable forests. The logging and manufacturing processes
are expected to conform to the environmental regulations
of the country of origin.

Jessica Kingsley Publishers
Carmelite House
50 Victoria Embankment
London EC4Y 0DZ

www.jkp.com

Contents

Acknowledgements

I have collected or devised the games and activities in this series of books over a 30-year period of working first as a speech and language therapist with children and adults, and then as a lecturer and workshop facilitator. Some were contributed by children during their participation in therapy groups or by teachers and therapists during workshops and discussions. Thank you!

The suggestions for adaptations and the expansion activities have arisen from my experiences of running children's groups. Many of them combine elements of ImageWork (Dr Dina Glouberman), Personal Construct Theory (see, for example, Peggy Dalton and Gavin Dunnett) and Solution-Focused Brief Therapy (Insoo Kim Berg and Steve de Shazer). My thanks therefore go to my teachers and mentors in these fields.

I have also found the following books helpful:

- Arnold, A. (1976) *The World Book of Children's Games*. London: Pan Books Ltd.
- Beswick, C. (2003) *The Little Book of Parachute Play*. London: Featherstone Education Ltd.
- Brandes, D. and Phillips, H. (1979) *Gamesters' Handbook: 140 Games for Teachers and Group Leaders*. London: Hutchinson.
- Dunn, O. (1978) *Let's Play Asian Children's Games*. Macmillan Southeast Asia in association with the Asian Cultural Centre for UNESCO.
- Liebmann, M. (2004) *Art Therapy for Groups: A Handbook of Themes and Exercises* (2nd edition). London and New York: Routledge.
- Masheder, M. (1989) *Let's Play Together*. London: Green Print.
- Neelands, J. (1990) *Structuring Drama Work: A Handbook of Available Forms in Theatre and Drama*. Cambridge: Cambridge University Press.

Note: Please remember, if you are a parent or carer and you are concerned about ongoing and persistently high levels of anxiety or low mood in a child, it is always best to seek further support via your child's school or your child's doctor. This book is not intended as a substitute for the professional help that may be needed when children are experiencing clinically recognized difficulties, such as chronic school phobia, severe social anxiety or childhood depression.

Wherever 'wellbeing' is used without further specification, this refers to social, psychological and emotional wellbeing.

As with any games involving the use of equipment, the parachute games outlined in this book should be supervised by an adult at all times.

The following icons are used throughout to indicate the three elements of the IMPACT approach:

Imagination

Mindful Play

Creative Thinking

Introduction

This book is one of a series based on the use of Imagination (I), Mindful Play (MP) and Creative Thinking (CT) to enhance social, psychological and emotional wellbeing and resilience in children. IMPACT activities and strategies encourage children to build life skills through carefully structured and supportive play experiences. Emphasis is given to the important role played by adult facilitators in creating a safe space in which children can share and explore feelings and difficulties and experiment with different ways of thinking and 'being'. This approach is explained in the accompanying eBook *Using Imagination, Mindful Play and Creative Thinking to Support Wellbeing and Resilience in Children*, which also contains many further ideas for games and activities and examples of how the IMPACT approach can enhance daily interactions with children.

USING THIS BOOK

The games and activities in this book help children to:

- identify their current strengths and skills
- explore ideas about what 'being confident' means
- understand how their skills of focusing and attending can help them to build self-confidence
- explore ways in which they can use the power of their own imagination to influence how they feel, think and act.

Facilitator involvement

All the games and activities in this series of books offer opportunities for facilitators to take an active part. Our participation reflects the nature of extended communities and gives us an opportunity to have fun alongside the children. Throughout the games in this book, the term 'game coordinator' therefore refers to either adult or child partici-pants, as appropriate for the level and stage of each group.

Activities

The first section of games and activities, Phase One: 'IMPACT Essentials for Build-ing Self-Confidence' (section II), introduces children to the central elements of the IMPACT approach – using imagery, being mindful and thinking creatively. There are also activities for group 'gelling' and for exploring relevant concepts such as self-respect and respect for others. Each book in the Helping Children to Build Well-being and Resilience series has a different set of IMPACT essentials. With a slight change of emphasis, you will be able to use any of these to supplement your sessions if needed.

The creative potential for supporting skill development is one of the wonderful features of childhood games. Play of this nature provides invaluable opportunities for children to learn through imitation, to experience the consequences of their actions and to experiment with different skills and different outcomes without fear of failure or being judged unfavourably by others. The multi-faceted nature of games means that in almost every game played there will be chances to enhance basic life skills, which, in turn, will help children to negotiate a variety of situations, now and in the future. I have given several suggestions for specific skills that might be learned or further developed during each game and its associated activities, but these are not exhaustive. You may want to add more to suit your own focus of work.

Ideas are also suggested for *adaptations*. These illustrate some of the many ways in which a basic game can be simplified or made more complex to suit diverse develop-mental levels, strengths and learning differences. This also means that IMPACT games and activities can be revisited several times, thus expanding each child's repertoire of appropriate skills and offering opportunities for choice and flexibility in how they initiate and participate in social interactions. Naturally, all the suggested activities and strategies in this book should be considered in light of your own training and the developmental levels, strengths and learning differences of the children you work with (see Chapter 12, 'Adapting Activities', in the accompanying eBook *Using Imagination, Mindful Play and Creative Thinking to Support Wellbeing and Resilience in Children*).

There are many different non-competitive 'mini' games that can be used for choosing groups, coordinators (leaders) and order of play where appropriate. I have listed several options in *Using Imagination, Mindful Play and Creative Thinking to Support Wellbeing and Resilience in Children* (see Chapter 14, 'Group Structures for Playing IM-PACT Games'). I suggest that the format is varied between sessions so that children can experiment with different ways of doing this. The choosing then becomes part of the social and personal learning.

Activity sheets

A selection of activity sheets can be found in section VI. These are marked with icons representing imagination and creative thinking. Of course, creative thinking and imagination are interrelated. This can also be a useful discussion point with children.

I have found that children particularly like to draw or write about their imaginary world. Their drawings and jottings might then be the starting point for wellbeing stories. (For ideas about how to create wellbeing stories, see Chapter 17, 'Image-Making and Wellbeing Stories', and Chapter 18, 'Helping Children to Create Their Own Wellbeing Stories', in *Using Imagination, Mindful Play and Creative Thinking to Support Wellbeing and Resilience in Children*.) They can also be made into a personal 'Book of Wisdom' and perhaps act as reminders of some of the strategies that children might want to use again in the future. There is a sample template for a 'Book of Wisdom' front cover at the start of section VI, 'Activity Sheets'.

Please keep in mind that the IMPACT activity sheets are offered as supplementary material to expand and reinforce each child's learning experiences. They are not intended as stand-alone alternatives to the mindful play and supportive discussions that are central to the IMPACT approach.

A PHASED APPROACH

This is the only activity book in the Helping Children to Build Wellbeing and Resilience series that offers session outlines for different phases of group work. While the IMPACT approach is just that – an approach rather than a programme – thinking about phases of support is particularly important for helping children to experience a gradual increase in self-confidence.[1]

I have suggested four phases rather than a set number of sessions, since the amount of time spent at each one may differ markedly according to the needs of the children, available resources and the size of the group.

These outlines combine extended and elaborated elements of *confidence groups* and the suggested format for a single IMPACT session, both of which can be found in

---

1   Some of the material in the suggested format for Phase One originally appeared in Plummer, D. (2015) 'Mindful Games.' In C. Willard and A. Saltzman (eds) *Teaching Mindfulness Skills to Kids and Teens* (Chapter 17). New York: Guilford Press.

the accompanying eBook *Using Imagination, Mindful Play and Creative Thinking to Support Wellbeing and Resilience in Children* – see Chapters 13, 14 and 15.

The games in each phase are followed by one or more *expansion activities*. These are an important part of the process too, and can be adapted for individual work or varying group sizes. They encourage children to recognize the benefits of a stepped approach to learning and to the process of change, understand how new skills can build on previous experiences, and how current skills can be strengthened. This also allows for increased flexibility in how the support phases are initiated and revisited. A summary list of activities is given for each phase to aid this process and to provide a reference point for your session plans.

You might also find it useful to add a selection of games and activities from *Helping Children to Manage Friendships* and *Helping Children to Build Communication Skills*, both of which are available in this series.

Over and beyond the suggested games and expansion activities I encourage you to use wellbeing stories and puppets during all four phases. There are many ideas in the accompanying eBook, and you will undoubtedly have many more of your own. Once the children are 'tuned in' to the benefits and enjoyment of their own imaginative abilities, and of mindful play and creative thinking, I'm sure you'll find that they are also able to contribute to the content of each phase, furthering their self-confidence and perceptions of self-efficacy even more.

Exploring Self-Confidence

A MINDFUL PLAY PERSPECTIVE

Self-confidence is one of the eight foundation elements explored in the IMPACT approach to supporting wellbeing and resilience in children (see Chapter 4, 'The Foundation Elements for Wellbeing', in *Using Imagination, Mindful Play and Creative Thinking to Support Wellbeing and Resilience in Children*). It is closely allied to the wellbeing foundation elements of *self-knowledge* and *self and others* and to a child's capacity for developing *self-reliance* and *self-acceptance*. Each of these elements is explored in a variety of ways throughout the games and activities in sections II–VI.

In the same way that we can talk about healthy self-esteem in contrast to high self-esteem (see Chapter 3, 'Wellbeing and Healthy Self-Esteem', in *Using Imagination, Mindful Play and Creative Thinking to Support Wellbeing and Resilience in Children*), we can also think of self-confidence as consisting of a healthy balance of belief in oneself, a realistic awareness of what is achievable, and vision in terms of the challenges that we can embrace and the obstacles that we can overcome. In 'healthy' self-confidence this transformational mixture of personal beliefs is profoundly linked to our relationship with others and to our awareness of the mutuality involved in these connections. This balance of autonomy and relationship is a vital element in helping children to understand and build self-confidence. It helps them to avoid or successfully negotiate possible future pitfalls such as false optimism or unrealistic confidence that could so easily be detrimental to their wellbeing and to the wellbeing of others. Non-competitive group games and discussions are an ideal vehicle for promoting this concept.

IMPACT activities explore aspects of group cooperation and trust, and aim to promote an understanding of how our thoughts and actions affect our relationships with other people. They aim to help children to identify with appropriate role models and to encourage the ability to work with or alongside other children and adults with awareness and empathy. Engagement in shared attention activities also helps children to direct their focus and concentration without being inappropriately distracted by others.

IMPACT activities also provide opportunities for supporting children in building self-reliance by actively promoting feelings of being in control, and by helping children in their growing abilities to anticipate and predict what might happen next, both as a consequence of their own behaviour and also as a consequence of other people's behaviour.

Helping children to build their self-confidence through games, activities and strategies involves helping them to experience a sense of being in control of their emotions, decisions and aspirations, and taking ownership of outcomes in a fun, experimental way without worries about failing or being judged. As a guide, we are fully present for each child. We take responsibility for the structure of the interaction – the pace, when it might be appropriate to move on, which activities might be most useful at which stage and for which children – and we facilitate the child's engagement with their natural problem-solving and goal-setting abilities. Supporting children in this way involves a great deal of trust on our part – trust in ourselves as guides and facilitators, and trust in the innate capacities of children that may just need to be re-awakened. It is an approach that has become embedded in many counselling practices and is particularly evident in motivational interviewing, which is widely used in healthcare settings.[1]

CONFIDENCE GROUPS

Genuine appreciation and constructive feedback from both adults and peers plays a large part in this process (see Chapter 13, 'Mindful Praise and Appreciation', in *Using Imagination, Mindful Play and Creative Thinking to Support Wellbeing and Resilience in Children*). This aspect has been specifically addressed in the phased approach outlined in this book by incorporating structured experiences of giving and receiving feedback in *confidence groups*. The idea for these groups is based on the format for *oekos*, or 'home', groups, which are an established element of ImageWork training, combined with aspects of techniques developed by Lee Glickstein[2] as a means of personal development

1   See, for example, Rollnick, S., Miller, W.R. and Butler, S.S. (2008) *Motivational Interviewing in Health Care*. New York and London: Guilford Press.
2   Glickstein, L. (1998) *Be Heard Now! Tap into Your Inner Speaker and Communicate with Ease*. New York: Broadway Books.

13

in public speaking. Glickstein's work is well known in the UK as a self-help tool for adults who stammer.

Speech and language therapists Carolyn Desforges, Louise Tonkinson and Suzie Kelly[3] also developed a particular version of this approach that can be used with children. I have taken some of the principles that they outline and have altered the format to create confidence groups. These groups aim to emphasize and promote existing skills as well as helping children to develop new skills. They promote connectedness within the group – giving children a forum in which to be heard by others, and the opportunity to learn how to give and receive acceptance and 'positive regard', thus contributing to the building of self-respect and respect for their peers (see Chapter 6, 'A Child-Centred, Mindful Approach', in *Using Imagination, Mindful Play and Creative Thinking to Support Wellbeing and Resilience in Children*).

Where you are working with large numbers of children, this is best facilitated by splitting into smaller groups. I have facilitated *confidence groups* with up to 12 children participating, but obviously the size of the group depends partly on the length of time available and the number of facilitators/helpers who know the format.

The format for each stage of the confidence groups is described in the relevant activities sections of this book.

EXPLORATORY ACTIVITIES

To get a feel for some of the activities and how these relate to a child's experiences of self-confidence, it is helpful to start from our own perspectives. How do we, as adults, view self-confidence? Is this different to the ways in which children view self-confidence? How do we already support the children in our care as they build their confidence? How can we maximize this support?

Experiencing the following explorations from an adult perspective will undoubtedly trigger some thoughts about how you can adapt these and other activities in this book. There are no right or wrong answers to any of these; they are simply ways of exploring the topic.

Begin by setting aside a short period of uninterrupted time when you will have the opportunity to carry out and reflect on a single activity – 10–15 minutes is probably

3   Desforges, C., Tonkinson, L. and Kelly, S. (2006) 'Using the power of speaking circles to develop confident communication.' *Speaking Out*, Spring, 6–7.

ample. I suggest that you only carry out one exploration and then go back to doing other things. Please don't be tempted to do all the activities one after the other in a single sitting, even if you have the time. A period of reflection is always useful after an exploration of this nature.

Exploratory activity 1.1. Indications of confidence

Bring to mind a child whom you consider to be self-confident. Ask yourself, 'How do they show that they are confident? How do they act? What sorts of things do they say about themselves?' Make a list of 10 skills, qualities, actions and ways of communicating that lead you to view this child as being self-confident.

Make a similar list for a child who appears to be low in self-confidence.

Does your second list consist of opposites of the first list, or are there any different/extra features? This will, of course, depend on the children you have chosen, but it is worth thinking about. A lack of self-confidence can present in a variety of ways, some of which are obvious (such as refusal to join in with group activities) and some that are more subtle (such as over-compliance with the wishes and preferences of a friend). These differences can be the basis for useful discussion points in some of the games and activities in this book.

SELF-EFFICACY AND MOTIVATION

Psychologists make a useful distinction between self-confidence and self-efficacy, seeing self-confidence as a general trait that colours all aspects of a person's life, and perceived self-efficacy as being a person's belief that they have control over certain outcomes that can be successfully performed (Bandura 1990).[4] In other words, self-efficacy is specific to tasks and situations and can be enhanced through personal accomplishment. We know from Dr Bandura's work that this can have far-reaching effects. He suggests that people who have perceptions of high self-efficacy often do better than those who

---

4   Bandura, A. (1990) 'Conclusion: Reflections on Nonability Determinants of Competence.' In R.J. Sternberg and J. Kolligian, Jr (eds) *Competence Considered* (pp.316–352). New Haven, CT: Yale University Press (cited in S. Harter (1999) *The Construction of the Self*. New York and London: Guilford Press).

have equal ability but less belief in themselves. They are more likely to persevere with difficult tasks, use more effective problem-solving strategies, set themselves more demanding goals and focus less on the possible consequences of failure. (See 'Skills and qualities' in Chapter 5, 'Making Experience Count', in *Using Imagination, Mindful Play and Creative Thinking to Support Wellbeing and Resilience in Children*.)

Self-efficacy can also be enhanced when a child sees someone else (particularly a peer) successfully tackle the same or similar task and perhaps struggle to begin with, but then overcome any difficulties ('Maybe if they can do it, then I can too'). Seeing another child enjoying their success and the benefits of this success can be an effective motivator.

Low efficacy levels can, of course, inhibit motivation. If a child feels that they have so far 'failed' in some way, then their sense of self-efficacy will be affected, and the more experience they have of this, the less they will want to try anything new.

Exploratory activity 1.2. Efficacy and motivation

Think of a (small) task that you are planning to undertake but you haven't started yet and perhaps don't feel particularly motivated to do so. How important is this task for you? On a scale of 1–5, where 1 is 'Not at all important' and 5 is 'Very important', where would you rate this task? How confident are you that you could complete this task if you did undertake it? Again, use a scale of 1–5, where 1 is 'Slightly confident' and 5 is 'Very confident'.

What generally motivates you to complete tasks (for example, personal satisfaction, a sense of achievement, being helpful to others)? Make a list of five possible motivators. On a scale of 1–5 rate each of your motivators in relation to its relevance to your chosen task, where 1 is 'Not very relevant' and 5 is 'Very relevant'.

Take a few moments to reflect on your responses.

Now do the same exercise with a child in mind, perhaps a child who appears not to be motivated to complete an assignment or to change their level of engagement in a class activity. Imagine yourself as this child. Sit in a different chair, adopt the child's posture and facial expression. Try to feel what it is like to be them. As this child, what would your ratings be for the task you have in mind?

When you have finished, make sure that you sit in your own chair and go back to being an adult!

The IMPACT approach is structured in a way that helps children to understand and develop or build on specific skills and strategies that will lead to actual competency, and to perceived self-efficacy, both of which are key elements of healthy self-confidence (see, for example, Chapter 5, 'Making Experience Count', and Chapter 11, 'Mindful Communication', in *Using Imagination, Mindful Play and Creative Thinking to Support Wellbeing and Resilience in Children*). They will be able to experiment with a variety of skills, take on progressively bigger challenges, be creative in constructing and trying out new games, take on different roles within games and cope with unexpected outcomes. The games and activities also help the children to recognize and celebrate their strengths, tolerate mild frustration and develop the capacity to recognize and accept supportive feedback from others. Exploring a range of appropriate strategies and becoming familiar with the language of problem-solving is also an important aspect of IMPACT activities.

While loss or lack of self-efficacy is usually experienced in relation to specific areas and for a specific reason, loss or lack of *self-confidence* is a pervasive experience of being unable to do anything with assurance. This is also related to perceptions of being 'in control'.

LOCUS OF CONTROL

Our sense of having a degree of control over different areas of our lives is influenced by our natural temperament, our culture and our lifetime experiences. Most children have very limited experiences of being in control. They are generally told what to do, think and say and when to do it. Learning to make decisions or to take responsibility for their actions is a slow and steady process. 'They made me do it' is perhaps a familiar cry heard by many of us! This is a natural part of growing up.

Gradually we will each develop different views about the amount of control we are able to exercise in our own lives. Some people develop a strong internal locus of control. They use language that reflects the belief that they are in control of their own fate: 'My achievements are due to my hard work.' They also use 'I' statements, rather than 'You' statements. For example, a statement such as 'You make me so angry' assumes a very different locus of control to 'I feel angry about what you just said/did'. Some people are more inclined to look externally for the reasons behind events in their life such as powerful others (health professionals, government and so on) or fate: 'It's just luck of the draw.'

The next exploratory activity offers an opportunity to look at this aspect of our lives and to think about its relevance for helping children to build self-confidence.

Exploratory activity 1.3. Life paths

Life path exercises are sometimes used in therapeutic and teaching work as a way to facilitate a review of important people, events and circumstances in a person's life. The explorer usually starts from birth or a key event in childhood, and works toward the present moment. In this activity you will approach the task slightly differently, tracing a path *backwards* from the present moment.[5]

Note: In order to avoid distractions, this exploration will be maximally effective if you read through the guidance a couple of times and then carry out the activity with your eyes closed. I suggest that you also have some paper and pencils close to hand.

Begin by thinking about something that you have recently achieved and which you feel positive about. Settle yourself in a comfortable position. Allow your eyes to close gently. Follow the normal pattern of your breathing for a moment... Notice the flow of air in and out of your body... Now let that focus fade...

Imagine yourself standing on a path that stretches ahead of you and behind you. This point represents the present moment. Imagine yourself looking back along the path at the journey you have already made. You may want to imagine an aerial view to help you with this. Take some time just to get a feel for the type of path that you have been following. Is it mostly rocky or mostly smooth? Perhaps it is hilly or flat, or a mixture of both. What can you see on the path? What can you see at the sides of the path?

Now imagine yourself walking back along the path to a point that represents a relatively recent time – this could be a few days or perhaps a month ago. Pause and imagine that you are there, in that time. In other words, you are not just remembering what was happening a few days or a month ago; you are experiencing it as if it is happening now. Remind yourself that you are exploring a positive achievement, something that you feel good about.

Ask yourself, 'What is happening at this point? What are my thoughts? What is the attitude that got me to this point? What is my strongest feeling?'

5   See Glouberman, D. (2003) *Life Choices, Life Changes: Develop Your Personal Vision with Imagework* (revised edition). London: Hodder & Stoughton; Glouberman, D. (2014) *You Are What You Imagine*. London: Watkins Publishing.; Glouberman, D. (2022) *ImageWork*. Monmouth: PCCS Books.

When you are ready, open your eyes and draw or note down what you were doing and what was happening on the path at that time.

When you feel that you have a sense of what was happening a month ago, take a longer view, perhaps two months, or even six months. Keep doing this until you have identified several points along the path that you feel have influenced your current achievements, decisions and attitudes. At each stage, remind yourself that you are experiencing this, not as a memory, but 'as if' it is actually happening.

When you have explored as much of the path as feels comfortable for you, imagine yourself walking back to the point at which you started – to the present moment. From this perspective, if you could whisper something to the you of a few months ago, what would you whisper?

When you are ready, open your eyes and bring yourself fully back to the room. You might do this by moving your feet to feel the solidity of the floor or simply shift your position and have a stretch. When you feel fully present within the room, draw or write about your path. Please do this before you talk to anyone about it.

Thinking about a life path, with specific emphasis on what has influenced your current choices, can be illuminating in itself and you may not feel the need to explore this any further. If you do want to think about it in more depth, however, here are some questions that I have found helpful:

- How much did I feel in control of the choice that I made?
- At any point, did I have other choices, other paths that I could take?
- What factors influenced my choice of this particular path at each significant point?
- How much do I feel in control of the way in which I proceed along the path into the future?
- Were there any key helpers or mentors for me along the way? How might I draw on my own strengths and on the help of others in the future?
- Am I aware of the factors contributing to any noticeably smooth or rough areas of the path? For example, was it smooth/rough because of outside influences, because of my own attitude/emotions or due to a combination of factors? How might this inform my future choices?

Life path images are not always clear or obvious metaphors but they can be a useful starting point for further exploration and can lead to important moments of insight. A simplified version of this activity can also be used with children to help them to formulate their goals and to feel more confident about achieving them. (See, for example, 'Exploratory activity 9.4. Taking steps' and the example of Andrew and Marcus both of which are in Chapter 9 of *Using Imagination, Mindful Play and Creative Thinking to Support Wellbeing and Resilience in Children*.)

FOCUSING AND CALMING

Feelings of control are also linked to the ability to focus and to self-calm. IMPACT games, activities and strategies aim to help children to recognize times when they are able to focus and concentrate successfully and to acknowledge times when this might be difficult, perhaps because of distracting internal thoughts and feelings (especially when these are self-limiting thoughts such as 'I can't do this') or external circumstances (such as a noisy environment over which they have no control). Activities also aim to enhance positive body awareness so that children can, for example, let go of unwanted tension or focus on calm breathing, and can learn to use body awareness to further develop their capacity for being mindful and to build self-confidence.

PHYSICAL ACHIEVEMENTS

We know that succeeding at a challenging physical endeavour can be very rewarding and can greatly contribute to a child's self-confidence. It is not within the scope of this book to cover the type of active play that involves physical achievements such as climbing or negotiating obstacle courses, but most games do involve coordination and balance and can often be adapted for play outside. Noticing and commenting on physical achievements during games will be an important part of the facilitator's role, and we can also encourage children to tell us about achievements such as climbing a tree, swimming two lengths of the pool, or negotiating difficult terrain on a bicycle.

IMAGINATION, SELF-CONFIDENCE AND CREATIVITY

The connections that we make between imagination and creativity also often depend on feelings of confidence. For instance, although I might consider myself to be imaginative, my aim of becoming more creative in my interactions with a child could be influenced by how confident I feel in my own creative abilities, my confidence in the intrinsic efficacy of the activities I have chosen, and my level of confidence in my knowledge of the child.

Some time ago I helped out at a regular family craft session run in the local community hall. I offered puppet making as one of the tabletop activities. During the first session we used wooden spoons, paints and a basket full of scraps of material and wool. Parents and grandparents took part to varying degrees. Some made the puppets for their children, following the child's instructions as to where to paint the eyes, what colour wool to use for the hair, and so on. Others sat next to their child and gently encouraged or helped when asked. Some parents made their own puppet alongside their child.

For some parents and grandparents it was a liberating experience; others found it daunting. A few remarked that they hadn't done any sticking and painting since their own childhood. One parent said that she didn't want to make a puppet because she was not creative enough. This was not what I had hoped for a family craft session. This experience once again highlighted some of the many ways in which mindful games and activities can influence each participant's sense of self-efficacy and their level of motivation to engage.

So, while we still needed an overall structure or theme (complete freedom to do whatever you want can also feel overwhelming and inhibiting for some people), subsequent sessions became much more free-flowing and creative. We would pile up a selection of various materials and see what children came up with in association with a general theme, such as animals and birds, or heroes and heroines. One child wanted to make a flapping bird and another child's father showed us how to fold the paper wings. Someone's big sister showed us how to add a weight to a paper snake to make it move like a puppet.

The table became a buzz of conversation between parents and children, and there was no thought of getting things 'right'. We were just using our imaginations freely, experimenting, and playing to strengths. Participants took 'ownership' of the outcomes. The result was that the children often went home with much more inventive, creative puppets than during the first session. On the other hand, there were one or two children who made wooden spoon puppets every session until they had a small family of them, each with its own unique character. It was just as important that they were able to choose to do this.

In summary, the IMPACT approach to helping children to build self-confidence involves engaging with children in imaginative and mindful play in order to encourage, support and honour their personal sense of efficacy and motivation.

The approach recognizes the central role played by peers and key adults in the development of each child's self-concept and potential for personal growth. It encourages creativity and experimentation in a safe and supportive environment and provides opportunities for children to acknowledge their strengths and challenges and to give and receive supportive feedback.

Children are also encouraged to transfer their growing confidence to real life situations and to recognize and celebrate their own progress and the progress of others.

Phase One: IMPACT Essentials for Building Self-Confidence

AIMS

- To give children information about how the group will run.
- To begin to establish group rapport.
- To help children to identify current strengths.
- To begin the exploration of imagination, being mindful and thinking creatively.
- To introduce stage 1 of the confidence groups (see 'Expansion activity 1.1. Remembering names').

SUGGESTED FORMAT AND NOTES

1. Pause to breathe: Ask the children to sit quietly in the space designated for the activities. Ask them to be as still as possible. This request is just setting up a 'pause' in thought and action. It is often helpful to give children specific instructions about how to achieve this. For example, show them how to be aware of their normal breathing and to feel the air as they breathe in and out, encourage them to listen to a specific sound or have them imagine that they are breathing in and breathing out each colour of the rainbow in turn (see 'Mindful breathing' in Appendix A of the accompanying eBook *Using Imagination, Mindful Play and Creative Thinking to Support Wellbeing and Resilience in Children*).

    Give positive feedback on how well all the group members are achieving this, noting the benefits to the group as a whole. For example, 'I am noticing how calm the group can be when you are doing relaxed breathing.'

Don't worry if there are some who find this aspect difficult. Some children will naturally become still and attentive within the space while others may take many weeks to get to this stage.

2. Explain: Explain the purposes of the group and give any information that is needed about timings, breaks and choosing to participate. (See 'Rules for games' in Chapter 14 of *Using Imagination, Mindful Play and Creative Thinking to Support Wellbeing and Resilience in Children.*) '3. I to eye' and 'Expansion activity 4.1. Wisdom rules!' provide children with an opportunity to think about more general group rules and guidance for the confidence groups, so you do not necessarily need to discuss these at this point.

3. Introduce: Introduce your chosen game/activity. Make the focus of the game explicit where appropriate. For example, you might introduce the game '1. Signs and signatures' by telling the children that it is a game for getting to know each other better. Wherever appropriate, tell the children what you are going to do, and how and why you are doing it, and invite any questions: 'We're going to play a focusing game. We need to sit in a circle. I will tell you/show you how to play. Do you want to ask me about the focusing game?' or 'Today we are going to play a game called "sense tracking". This game is about being mindful.'

It is important to make clear the skills being taught and reinforced, and to openly invite questions and personal insights from the children throughout all the activities.

4. Describe: Describe the game or activity briefly, making its rules, roles and time frame explicit. Keep instructions concrete, short and simple. If the activity involves the need to be particularly quiet, make this clear and give the reason. For example: 'When we taste the raisins, we are going to do it without talking so that we can make/keep a quiet space.'

5. Play: Play the game or carry out the activity. Sit quietly for a few moments afterwards so that the children can wind down and absorb what they have been doing.

6. 'Talk about' and/or drawing time: Each game will be maximally effective if the children have the chance to reflect on what happened. This reflective aspect may

range from a brief discussion or drawing activity about the general experiences of a game to more in-depth discussions about what was felt, learned and 'intuited' during and after the process of playing a game. To aid this process, I have included some suggestions ('Talk about'). These include a mixture of possible prompt questions and suggestions for comments or explanations that can be useful when introducing or elaborating some of the ideas.

Although it is helpful to have a few prompt questions prepared to ease the discussion, I would always recommend encouraging children's initial personal reflections too, however basic or brief or elaborate they might be. You may want to simply ask for a show of hands in response to a few key questions, such as 'Who feels that they are listening more mindfully?' or 'Who feels that they have learned something new about being confident?'

Group discussions should be centred on the understanding that nothing that anyone offers during these times can be 'wrong'. Children need to know that all insights, thoughts, questions and personal images will be respected. Unconditional acceptance and genuine constructive feedback in response to these insights will help them to learn, and to grow in confidence and motivation.

Discussion topics also provide an opportunity for drawing links between different themes at later times. You could remind children of particular games when this is relevant: 'Do you remember when we played that game of...? What did you find out about focusing attention?' or 'How might the mindful breathing activity be useful to us in this situation?' During all discussions it is helpful to use language that reflects the assumption that children are already doing something (however small) that will help them to build their self-confidence. For more ideas about facilitating discussions with children, see Chapter 11, 'Mindful Communication', and Chapter 13, 'Mindful Praise and Appreciation', in *Using Imagination, Mindful Play and Creative Thinking to Support Wellbeing and Resilience in Children*.

Repeat steps 3–6 with a new game or an expansion activity as appropriate for the timings and ability levels of the group.

7. Close: Thank the children for their participation and give brief positive feedback.
   Finish with an affirming comment to the whole group about your own experience of sharing the space with them. For instance, 'Thank you. I really enjoyed our time together.'
   Make a link with the next task for the day. Move quietly out of the space.

SUMMARY OF GAMES AND ACTIVITIES FOR PHASE ONE

1. **Signs and signatures**
   Expansion activities:
   > 1.1. Remembering names
   >
   > 1.2. Name associations

   Themes: Group gelling and creative thinking

2. **Sense tracking**
   Expansion activities:
   > 2.1. Tasting raisins
   >
   > 2.2. Green space sensing
   >
   > 2.3. Mindful focusing

   Theme: Being mindful

3. **I to eye**
   Expansion activity:
   > 3.1. Me and you

   Themes: listening and maintaining eye contact; stage 1 of confidence groups

4. **Parachute creatures**
   Expansion activities:
   > 4.1. Wisdom rules!
   >
   > 4.2. Spaceship to the stars

   Themes: group cooperation; imagination; group rules

5. **Adverts**
   Expansion activities:
   > 5.1. Achievements
   >
   > 5.2. Word puzzles

   Themes: exploring skills and creative thinking

1. Signs and signatures

Wellbeing focus:

☑ Self-confidence

Examples of personal skills learned or consolidated:

☑ Listening
☑ Concentration
☑ Memory strategies
☑ Taking turns

☑ Observation
☑ Understanding and using non-verbal communication

Examples of general/social learning:

☑ Appreciating diversity
☑ Building self-respect and respect for others

☑ Exploring self-concept

How to play

Players sit in a circle. The first player says their name accompanied by a movement/gesture (such as a head movement, clapping, making a sweeping gesture with both hands). The next person introduces the previous player (using their name and gesture) and then says their own name accompanied by their own gesture.

This is _____ and I am _____

Finish with everyone saying and gesturing their own name at the same time.

Adaptations

- Teach the children specific signs, such as finger spelling for their initials or signs for different animals or objects so that each child can say their name and then sign an animal or object of their choice.
- Players say their own name and think of a gesture, but do not need to introduce anyone.

- Play the game standing up and include large movements such as jump back, shake leg, hop.
- In smaller groups players can try and remember the names and gestures of as many previous players as possible.

Talk about

If you had a different name, would you choose a different gesture? Do you think other people would link this gesture with your name?

Think of a family member or a friend. What gesture might they choose to go with their name? Would you choose a different gesture for them or the same one?

Experiment with several famous names and see if the group can come to an agreement about the appropriate type of movement to associate with each name (such as a royal wave or a fist pump).

EXPANSION ACTIVITY 1.1. REMEMBERING NAMES

Players sit in a circle. The game coordinator throws a soft cushion around the group. Each person says their own name when they catch it. After everyone has had a turn, go round again. This time the rest of the group say the name of the person who catches the cushion. (Use a weighted or strangely shaped soft object so that everyone is likely to have some difficulty catching it – a fun way to even out the ability levels in the group.)

Adaptation

For groups that already know each other you could substitute their real names for famous people or for middle names.

Talk about

Names are an important part of who we are. You may have chosen to shorten your name or use a nickname. We can show respect for others by remembering to use their preferred name. How do you help yourself to remember people's names? Do you have any special ways of remembering that you could share with the group?

EXPANSION ACTIVITY 1.2. NAME ASSOCIATIONS

Children are offered one way of remembering names, which is to make a link with something else, such as a colour that they like to wear (use activity sheet 1.2). This could also be done by asking everyone to come up with a way that they would like to be described, using adjectives beginning with the first letter of their name, for example 'Cool Cathy', 'Stylish Stuart', 'Relaxed Rajeev'. Or you could introduce the use of imagery at this stage by suggesting that children think of an image that they associate with each person in the group. This could be literal, such as Rajeev relaxing in an armchair, or metaphorical, such as Rajeev as a sleeping cat.

2. Sense tracking

Wellbeing focus:

☑ Self-confidence

Examples of personal skills learned or consolidated:

☑ Focusing attention   ☑ Memory strategies
☑ Concentration   ☑ Taking turns

Examples of general/social learning:

☑ Building persistence   ☑ Developing flexibility of thought
☑ Extending awareness

How to play

This version of a traditional 'I spy' game encourages children to use all their senses and their imagination.

The game coordinator provides a tray of different foods and items with a variety of different textures, sounds and smells (at least 20 items). The whole group is shown the tray uncovered for 30 seconds. The tray is then covered with a cloth.

The children are reminded that some objects can probably be identified using more than one sense (see the examples below).

Player A looks under the cloth and starts off the game, naming any sense as appropriate.

(Of course, 'I spy' will be appropriate for all the objects, so this can be disallowed if you want!)

For example:

I can hear something beginning with 'b' (Bell? Bouncing ball? Balloon that has been popped?)

I can smell something beginning with 'c' (Crisp? Chocolate? Crayons?)

I can feel something beginning with 'm' (Mud? Marmalade? Mushy peas?)

I can taste something beginning with 'm' (Mud? Marmalade? Mushy peas?)

Whoever guesses correctly takes the next turn.

The game will naturally get easier the longer it is played as everyone begins to remember what is under the cloth.

Talk about

How do you feel after playing this game?

Was it easy or difficult to keep concentrating on the game? Why was this?

What sort of things made it easier/harder for you to listen/observe/concentrate?

Which sense do you think you use the most?

When you close your eyes for a while, do you hear sounds that you hadn't noticed before (such as the clock ticking)?

Do you like to try new food that you've never tasted before? What is the difference between eating and tasting?

How might learning to focus our attention also help us to build self-confidence? For example, when might it be useful to focus away from our thoughts and focus on our breathing instead? How might focusing on, listening to, or observing something in nature help us when we are feeling anxious? Does the ability to change our focus of attention from one thing to another help us when we are trying to complete a challenging task? Is this true for everyone? Why do you think this? (See 'Expansion activity 2.3.' and also Chapter 7, 'Helping Children to be Mindful', in the accompanying eBook *Using Imagination, Mindful Play and Creative Thinking to Support Wellbeing and Resilience in Children*).

EXPANSION ACTIVITY 2.1. TASTING RAISINS

Dr Jon Kabat-Zinn, founder of the Stress Reduction Clinic at the University of Massachusetts Medical Center, describes an exercise where adult participants are asked to eat three raisins, one at a time, 'paying attention to what we are actually doing and experiencing from moment to moment' (Kabat-Zinn 1990, p.27).[1] This is a lovely activity to do with children too (but have an alternative food to hand in case anyone doesn't like raisins!). It gives them an opportunity to focus their attention in a fun way and to talk

---

1   There is a detailed explanation of this exercise in Dr Kabat-Zinn's book Full *Catastrophe Living* (revised and updated edition 2020, pp.15–16, London: Piatkus). See also Umass Memorial Health Center for Mindfulness (www.ummhealth.org/center-mindfulness).

about it afterwards just as an experience – there is no possibility of doing it in the wrong way, even if they eat the raisins all at once and very quickly. They will simply have a different, but equally valid, experience.

How to play

Ask the children to first bring their attention to 'seeing' the raisin, then to feel the texture and to notice the colours and smell of the raisin. They might also be aware of any thoughts that they have about raisins and food in general.

Encourage them to notice the movement of their hand to their mouth, and the touch of the raisin on their lips or tongue, notice the taste, and notice how they feel once they have eaten the raisin.

Repeat this three times. After a brief period of stillness, invite the children to talk about what happened.

In an interview with Bill Moyers, Dr Kabat-Zinn describes what happens with adult participants:

'In this exercise, people realize, "My goodness, I never taste raisins. I'm so busy eating them that I don't actually taste them." From there, it's a very short jump to realize that you may actually not be in touch with many of the moments of your life, because you're so busy rushing someplace else that you aren't in the present moment...you may be tuning out of all sorts of inner and outer experiences simply because you're too preoccupied with where you want to get, what you want to have happen, and what you don't want to happen... Once we do the raisin exercise, people begin to realize that there's nothing magical about mindfulness.'[2]

EXPANSION ACTIVITY 2.2. GREEN SPACE SENSING

Play sense tracking outside, referring to all the senses to guess different elements in the environment. In this version the facilitator first collects items from the environment, such as seed pods that rattle, fallen twigs that feel rough or smooth, leaves that feel hairy or smooth, etc. Of course, children

---

2   Kabat-Zinn, J. (1993) 'Meditation.' In B. Moyers (ed.) *Healing and the Mind*. London: Aquarian/Thorsons, pp.117–118.

could also be taken on a nature walk to collect the items, but unless you are doing this in a well-maintained community space, this will naturally need to be well supervised to avoid inadvertent collection of poisonous plants or irritants. An alternative would be for children to sit in a circle in a green space and observe/listen/feel everything around them, such as the sound of rustling leaves, the feel of the grass where they are sitting, or the 'tickle' of the breeze.

EXPANSION ACTIVITY 2.3. MINDFUL FOCUSING

Invite the children to practice swapping their focus of attention from listening to the sounds around them for 30 seconds to being aware of their own breathing for the same amount of time.

Then ask them to swap from listening to music to noticing the sensations in their feet or hands (while the music is still playing).

Was this easy or difficult to do? Why was that? Talk about how consciously changing the focus of our attention can help us to feel more confident. For example, we can notice and rename physical sensations if appropriate – 'This isn't anxiety, it's excitement' – or shift from internal thoughts that are unhelpful to external circumstances and back again in order to do 'a reality check'.

3. I to eye

Wellbeing focus:

☑ Self-confidence

Examples of personal skills learned or consolidated:

☑ Focusing attention   ☑ Memory strategies
☑ Listening   ☑ Taking turns
☑ Self-control   ☑ Eye contact

Examples of general/social learning:

☑ Building persistence   ☑ Extending awareness

This game is also in *Helping Children to Build Communication Skills*. Here, the emphasis on the combination of listening, self-control and eye contact is used as a way to begin discussions about how we can show support and connect with others through sensitive listening and appropriate body language. This discussion will facilitate the children's engagement with 'Expansion activity 3.1. Me and you', which is the first stage of the confidence groups.

How to play

This is a surprisingly complex version of a warm-up or group gelling game that can cause great hilarity if played mindfully. Players sit or stand in a circle. The game coordinator starts the game by gaining eye contact with another player and then saying their *own* name.

The coordinator and the other player swap places silently. The second player then gains eye contact with a third player and says their own name before swapping places (in other words, they do not need to know the names of other players).

The game continues until every player has said their own name. As players get to know each other, the tendency is to say someone else's name instead of their own. In this instance it is up to the named person to stay still.

Talk about

In preparation for 'Expansion activity 3.1. Me and you', the children are introduced to the three principles that will help the confidence groups to work well. They are encouraged to think about and discuss the following:

- Focus on the positive: When we take part in the groups, whether we are giving or receiving feedback, we remember to focus on our own and each other's skills rather than what we didn't do or what was 'missing'.
- The group members offer support to the speaker: What does 'giving support' mean? How can we show that we are supporting someone when they take part in the confidence groups? Think about how we can do this silently (for example, by fully listening and maintaining eye contact), and how we can show our support and acceptance verbally.
- The speaker 'connects' with the audience: How might keeping eye contact and breathing calmly help us to feel confident? How does eye contact help us to 'connect' with other people in the group? How does calm breathing help us to make this connection?

EXPANSION ACTIVITY 3.1. ME AND YOU (STAGE 1 OF CONFIDENCE GROUPS)

The children sit in a circle and are invited to relax and to become 'still' (see the notes for 'Pause to breathe' earlier). When they are ready, ask them to close their eyes and to notice what their body is feeling. Then, with eyes still closed, ask them to become aware of the other children in the group – sensing their presence in the circle. They then 'tune into' their own breathing again, and after a few moments forget about their breathing, open their eyes and then they are ready for the first confidence group activity.

The first round in the group doesn't involve any speaking at all. Instead, the children each take a turn to walk up to the 'stage' (a pre-chosen space in the circle). They make slow eye contact with each of the group members in the 'audience', and then walk back to their seat. The audience return eye contact and silently 'send' their complete acceptance. The 'speaker' is asked to be open to receive this acceptance. The children are encouraged to both sense the acceptance from their audience and to be aware of physical ways in which this is shown. This may seem a difficult concept for some at first, but they can be reassured that there is no right or wrong way of doing this.

When the child has returned to their seat, specific, truthful feedback is given by the group facilitators on looking confident, walking in a confident way, using calm breathing to settle themselves, gaining support by using eye contact, etc. The same format can be used with the children remaining seated and taking turns around the circle if this is more appropriate.

During this activity, facilitators are modelling the sort of feedback that will be appropriate for children to give to each other at a later time. There are specific games and activities that will help children to further explore the link between body language and confidence in 'Phase Three: What Is Confidence?'

4. Parachute creatures

(A long piece of fabric, such as a colourful sari, will also work well for this game.)

Wellbeing focus:

☑ Self-confidence

Examples of personal skills learned or consolidated:

☑ Giving instructions ☑ Cooperation
☑ Physical coordination

Examples of general/social learning:

☑ Being part of a group ☑ Understanding how and why
☑ Development of body awareness   rules are made
   and positive body image ☑ Understanding how individual
☑ Building group cohesion   behaviour affects others
☑ Building trust

As with all games involving the use of equipment, parachute games need to be supervised by an adult. This 'rule' can be a useful prompt for a discussion about group rules and why some rules are needed for safety reasons (see the discussion points below, in 'Talk about').

How to play

Players divide into teams and are given the task of constructing a mythical creature or a giant version of a mini beast using a parachute or cloth and a ball of string. They are told that they must somehow make their creature move across a large space (for example, across the playground or room).

   (Hopefully at least one of the teams will drape the cloth over themselves and walk in a line, but they will need to cooperate and they will need to have a leader.)

Talk about

How did you work out what to do? Did different teams think of different ideas?

In this game you used your imagination. What is the best thing about being able to imagine something that doesn't really exist?

Can you imagine eating your favourite food? How do you feel when you imagine that? Can you imagine what it would be like to be an ant in a forest? What about if you were a bear?

What does 'being creative' mean? How can the ability to imagine help you to be creative? How could it help you to feel confident?

You didn't have many instructions for this game. What did you feel when you started? What do you feel now?

What were the rules for this game? Do all games have rules? Why do you think this? What are some of the rules that help to make a game feel safe?

How do you find out about the different rules for different groups?

What rules shall we have for this group?

EXPANSION ACTIVITY 4.1. WISDOM RULES!

Suggest to the children that they write a list of rules/guidelines for the group (using activity sheet 4.1). Use this to start (or add to) their personal 'Book of Wisdom' or start a shared 'Book of Wisdom' for the whole group. The activity sheet does not have any further instructions for children and can be used for different purposes. For example, group rules, personality safety 'rules' for building confidence, or writing about alternatives to the use of 'rules' such as 'preferred behaviour' or 'guidelines' (see 'Talk about' for 4. Parachute creatures).

EXPANSION ACTIVITY 4.2. SPACESHIP TO THE STARS

This activity can be found in Appendix B of the accompanying eBook *Using Imagination, Mindful Play and Creative Thinking to Support Wellbeing and Resilience in Children* and in *Helping Children to Manage Transitions*, another book in this series.

Introducing an imagery activity such as 'Spaceship to the stars' can be a useful way of helping children to identify and explore their goals. This also links with the following activity, '5. Adverts', as well as 'Expansion activity 5.1. Achievements' and '12. Cinema sensation'. These activities indicate to the children that they already have skills that will help them to build confidence, and choices about how and when to use and extend these skills. This is an important aspect of the IMPACT approach, and features in other games throughout this series of books. (See, for example, 'Exploratory activity 5.3. Skills and qualities' in *Using Imagination, Mindful Play and Creative Thinking to Support Wellbeing and Resilience in Children*.)

5. Adverts

Wellbeing focus:

☑ Self-confidence

Examples of personal skills learned or consolidated:

☑ Giving instructions   ☑ Cooperation

Examples of general/social learning:

☑ Being part of a group   ☑ Understanding how individual
☑ Building group cohesion   behaviour affects others
☑ Building trust

This game can also help children to recognize and explore some of the skills and attributes they have in relation to different aspects of their lives. There is no 'Talk about' section since the process itself will engender discussion during the activity.

How to play

Each player chooses a 'role' from a provided list. This could be a role that they actually play in life or one that they would like to play. This works best if at least three children choose each role. Players are then grouped together according to their choices, and cooperate to design a joint poster or TV advert for themselves in this role, highlighting skills and attributes. Volunteers share their posters in the circle.

Possible roles might be sports ace, computer expert, brother/sister, son/daughter, friend, artist, science whiz kid, inventor, builder.

Adaptations

- Instead of providing a list, facilitate a group discussion about possible roles.
- Players design 'Your class/group/community needs you' posters highlighting attributes and skills needed for successful group work.

EXPANSION ACTIVITY 5.1. ACHIEVEMENTS

The children spend some time drawing six stars and/or planets on activity sheet 5.1. These need to be large enough for them to be able to write a word or draw a small picture inside. Each child identifies something that they feel they have achieved recently. This could be related to school, home, friendships or a hobby. They write this achievement in the first star or planet on the activity sheet.

The achievements are shared in the group (the children have a choice about whether or not to contribute to this sharing, but are encouraged to sit with the group, even if they prefer not to say anything about their own achievement).

The children then talk about their aims for your mindful play sessions together. Some questions that you might like to explore are:

- Do you set yourself goals to work towards?
- What would you most like to achieve by the end of next week? Next month? Next term?
- How will you know when you've achieved it? How will other people know that you've achieved it?
- On a scale of 1–5, where 1 is 'I'm just starting' and 5 is 'I'm almost there', how far have you already gone towards achieving your goal?

The aims are collated and written up for everyone to see. Although the children might suggest a mixture of realistic aims and some that are not achievable within the time that you spend together, these can be discussed so that they can choose which aims to focus on.

In each subsequent session the facilitators and children remind themselves of the different aims on the list and notice, praise and record achievements accordingly. (See Chapter 13, 'Mindful Praise and Appreciation', in *Using Imagination, Mindful Play and Creative Thinking to Support Wellbeing and Resilience in Children*.)

Extra sheets of stars and planets are added at a later time if needed, and in accordance with how many sessions you are planning for the group.

EXPANSION ACTIVITY 5.2. WORD PUZZLES

(See also 'Expansion activity 10.3. Puzzles')

As a group, make up a riddle or poem using the letters of 'confidence' or an associated concept. Alternatively, you could provide puzzles for groups of children to decipher. For example:

> My first is in **C**heer but not in tease, my second is in th**O**ughtful and also in **O**pen-minded (and so on).

Or, for younger children:

> I know that a clue to the magic that's here can be found, if you look, at the start of a **C**heer, at the start of **O**urselves, at the start of each **N**ight, at the beginning of **F**riendships and Impish **D**elight, at the start of **E**xcitement, at the end of some fu**N**, add the middle of pea**CE**ful and now I have done.[3]

Or, think of an acrostic (where the letters of one word are used as the first letters of related words). For example:

Coolheaded
Attentive
Looking/listening
Mindful

---

3   Plummer, D. (1998) *Using Interactive Imagework with Children: Walking on the Magic Mountain.* London: Jessica Kingsley Publishers.

Phase Two: Self-Knowledge and Self-Acceptance

AIMS

- To strengthen group support and trust.
- To introduce the children to the second stage of the confidence groups.
- To explore self-knowledge and self-acceptance and how these link with self-confidence.

Here is a brief reminder of these two wellbeing foundation elements.

Self-knowledge

This is about developing an understanding of who 'I' am and where I fit into family, friendship and community groups. A secure sense of self and a sense of belonging both contribute to a child's level of self-confidence, and are vital elements of wellbeing.

Self-acceptance

Recognizing personal strengths and achievements and being able to accept sincere praise and compliments (aspects that are specifically facilitated by the confidence groups) are important aspects of self-acceptance. This element also involves recognizing what can't be changed and areas of personal difficulty that may require the development or refining of skills, understanding the difference between experimenting and failing, and developing and maintaining body awareness and positive body image.

SUGGESTED FORMAT AND NOTES

1. Pause to breathe (see notes for Phase One).

2. Brief check-in time: The children sit in a circle and briefly say how they are feeling today, or something they enjoyed about the previous session, or something they have noticed about themselves since the last session.

3. First praises and praise card(s) given: See 'Being specific' in Chapter 13 of the accompanying eBook *Using Imagination, Mindful Play and Creative Thinking to Support Wellbeing and Resilience in Children*. Each child in the group is congratulated or praised for something noted by facilitators in the previous session, reported as a noticeable change by someone else (such as a teacher, parent or another group member), or reported as an achievement by the child. One or more children, according to the size of the group, is also given a praise card agreed on by the other group members earlier, preferably out of hearing of the recipient. These cards are only given once to each child, and all members of the group receive one well before the completion of Phase Four (so no one has to wait until the last session of the group to receive their praise card).

4. Play the first game.

5. Brief feedback/'Talk about' time.

6. Second activity or game.

7. Longer 'Talk about' and/or drawing time.

8. Confidence group stages 1 and 2; stage 2 is also used for the closing activity (according to number of sessions intended for this phase): For confidence group stage 1, continue with stage 1 (see 'Expansion activity 3.1. Me and you'), but this time the facilitators *and* the children give feedback. The facilitators then have the opportunity to praise the children for their positive feedback.

    For confidence group stage 2/closing activity, the children take turns to walk up to the speaker position. They give and receive natural, gentle eye contact to everyone in turn, and can then choose whether to say one small sentence. They could perhaps say something that they like, or they could just say 'hello' before returning to their chairs. This time feedback is given primarily from group members with a small amount of feedback from the facilitators. The facilitators once again praise the children for the content and quality of the positive feedback given.

In this phase the children also gradually work towards using the confidence group in a closing activity, contributing one brief thought about the session(s) before they leave. For example:

I feel...

Today I found out that...

My name is...and I am...

I have noticed that...

I feel really good about...

I want to say that...

Today this group has given me...

Adaptations

- Use emotion pictures as prompts. The children choose the picture that best matches how they feel about the session.
- Offer possibilities based on your observations, for example 'Today I think you felt very proud of how well you did. Am I right?' or 'I noticed that today you really enjoyed telling us about your name story'.

SUMMARY OF GAMES AND ACTIVITIES FOR PHASE TWO

6. **This is me**

   Expansion activities:

   > 6.1. Is this me?
   >
   > 6.2. Create
   >
   > 6.3. Portraits
   >
   > 6.4. If I were an animal

   Themes: exploring personal attributes and skills; using imagery

7. **Story-line**

   Expansion activities

   > 7.1. The stories we tell (1)
   >
   > 7.2. Puppet play

   Theme: exploring personal history

8. **True or false?**

   Expansion activities:

   > 8.1. Three things I enjoy about myself
   >
   > 8.2. Skills
   >
   > 8.3. Loads of awards
   >
   > 8.4. Things I'm working on
   >
   > 8.5. Star turn

   Themes: imagination; acknowledging and celebrating current skills and challenges

9. **Colourful me**

   Expansion activity:

   > 9.1. The stories we tell (2)

   Themes: exploring talents and assets; constructing wellbeing stories

6. This is me

Wellbeing focus:

- ☑ Self-confidence

Examples of personal skills learned or consolidated:

- ☑ Understanding and using non-verbal communication
- ☑ Observation

Examples of general/social learning:

- ☑ Dramatic awareness
- ☑ Exploring self-concept
- ☑ Building self-respect and respect for others

How to play

Make a group list of positive words that can be used to describe a person's character, such as careful, friendly, creative. Remind the children about what is acceptable.

Write each positive word on a separate card. Now think of at least 10 actions and write each of these on separate cards as well.

Players take turns to pick an action and a characteristic from the two piles of cards, and attempt to do the action in the manner of the characteristic, for example 'Brush your hair carefully', 'Stroke a dog in a friendly way', 'Wave creatively!' The rest of the group try to guess the characteristic.

Adaptations

- In larger groups the children perform the actions in teams of threes or fours for everyone else to guess.
- Each child chooses one or more words from the list that could be used to describe their own personality, and then performs one of the actions.

Talk about

What does this game tell us about respecting ourselves and respecting others?

Ask the children to imagine how they might feel if they heard someone describing them in each of these ways. Is it okay to sometimes do or say something that is 'out of character'? For example, someone who is thoughtful might sometimes do something that is not thoughtful, but that doesn't mean that they are no longer a thoughtful person.

Do we show our main characteristics in everything we do? Do we show our main characteristics through action only?

EXPANSION ACTIVITY 6.1. IS THIS ME?

As a group, find and cut out descriptions of people from magazines and newspapers. These should be primarily positive and refer to attributes and skills rather than physical characteristics. Add just a handful of less appealing descriptions.

After discussing these descriptions, the children either choose some positive descriptions to paste onto their activity sheet (using activity sheet 6.1), or use them as a prompt for their own thoughts about how they would like to be described.

EXPANSION ACTIVITY 6.2. CREATE

Individually, or in pairs, the children choose five descriptions to use in a poem and present these to the group. This could be done now or during the confidence group activity in Phase Three.

EXPANSION ACTIVITY 6.3. PORTRAITS

The children draw or write about themselves in the portrait frame (using activity sheet 6.3). There are no further instructions on this activity sheet to allow for flexibility in how this is used. For example, children could also draw 'before', 'during' and 'after' portraits to indicate changes they have made during different phases of play.

EXPANSION ACTIVITY 6.4. IF I WERE AN ANIMAL

Lead the children in an imagery exercise. (See Chapter 8, 'Imagination and Images', and Chapter 9, 'Image-Making', in *Using Imagination, Mindful Play and Creative Thinking to Support Wellbeing and Resilience in Children*.)

Settle yourself comfortably on the floor or in your chair. When you are ready, close your eyes and take three full breaths, letting the air out slowly as you breathe out...

Imagine that you could be any animal you wanted. What would you be?

Now imagine that you *are* this animal... Step into being your chosen animal and really feel what that is like...

As this animal, do you make a sound? What sounds do you make?...

Do you move?... If so, *how* do you move?...

As this animal, where do you live?... What do you like doing?... What do you not like doing?...

What is the best thing about being you?...

What would you most like to be able to do?... What do you most wish for?...

Enjoy imagining being your chosen animal for a while.

When you are ready, open your eyes and draw or write about the animal that you chose.

Talk about

Invite the children to share feelings and insights related to their experience of 'being' their chosen animal.

7. Story-line

Wellbeing focus:

☑ Self-confidence

Examples of personal skills learned or consolidated:

☑ Listening
☑ Memory strategies
☑ Research skills

☑ Planning
☑ Sequencing/story-telling

Examples of general/social learning:

☑ Building self-respect and respect for others

☑ Appreciating diversity

Note: The children will need to do some research at home before this game can be played.

How to play

Players are given the task of researching their names in preparation for a subsequent session. Guide them with questions such as 'Do you know what your name means?', 'How was your name chosen?', 'How important is your name to you?', 'When you use your name, how do you use it?' and 'Do you like other people to use your full name or a shortened version, or do you have a favourite nickname?'

Players start by dividing into pairs to tell each other their name story (see ideas for choosing pairs in Chapter 14 of *Using Imagination, Mindful Play and Creative Thinking to Support Wellbeing and Resilience in Children*). Everyone then joins together in one circle and each player introduces their partner to the group and says one thing that they remembered about that person's story.

Adaptations

• Research middle names.

- When working with an individual or in smaller groups, take time to hear each child's full name story.
- Ask the children to research someone else's name – perhaps a sibling or parent.

Talk about

Was it easy or difficult to find out about your name? Did you learn anything about other people in your family that you didn't know already?

Do you have a name that is a 'family' name, given to successive generations, perhaps? What do you think about that? What did you find interesting about each other's name stories?

Do you associate some names with particular characteristics? Why might this happen?

Do you like to use a different name with your family and with your friends? If so, why?

Do you know anyone else with the same name as you? Are they anything like you, or are they very different?

EXPANSION ACTIVITY 7.1. THE STORIES WE TELL (1)

Individually, or as a group, construct fictional stories about how children were named (for example, in the style of a legend, a fairy story or a news item). Volunteers take turns to tell their story to the group or to tell their story to a facilitator who will then relay it to the group. Ideally all children should hear their story told aloud by an adult who is prepared to elaborate and exaggerate! If time is limited you may need to assure the children that they will be given this opportunity in other sessions.

Note: When children are telling stories about themselves it may be helpful to use objects or figures to give them something to hold and to focus on. A box full of lolly pop sticks is an invaluable tool for this. For example, children can draw a face on a stick or can make an animal face and tell their story as an animal (see 'Expansion activity 6.4. If I were an animal').

EXPANSION ACTIVITY 7.2. PUPPET PLAY

(See also expansion activity 9.1. The stories we tell (2))
As a group, make up a short puppet play about an animal or a mythical creature that doesn't have a name and sets off on an epic journey to find out who they really are.

What do they find out about themselves? What adventures do they have along the way?

Perform the play in small groups and/ or use the confidence group for players to share an insight gained during their construction of the play.

Finish with a discussion about what the children might take from this experience that will help them to build their own confidence.

For ideas about puppetry see Chapter 19, 'Using Puppets', in Using Imagination, Mindful Play and Creative Thinking to Support Wellbeing and Resilience in Children.

8. True or false?

Wellbeing focus:

☑ Self-confidence

Examples of personal skills learned or consolidated:

☑ Taking turns   ☑ Sharing personal information
☑ Listening   ☑ Initiating interactions

Examples of general/social learning:

☑ Building trust   ☑ Building self-respect and respect
                                for others

How to play
Everyone walks around the room introducing themselves to each other and saying two things about themselves. One of these is true and the other is false. Partners guess which is the false statement and which is the true one.

Adaptations

- In the circle, volunteers tell three amazing things about themselves, two of them false and one of them true. The group vote on which one is true.
- The children introduce themselves to one other person who then introduces them to the group, telling the amazing (true) fact.

Talk about
What is the difference between boasting and being proud of something? Are there any amazing true facts that you would like to celebrate with the group? What are some of the different *types* of amazing facts that people invented?

EXPANSION ACTIVITY 8.1. THREE THINGS I ENJOY ABOUT MYSELF

Players draw three things that they enjoy about themselves on a sheet of paper. They then pin this on their front and walk around the room to see what other children have drawn and to talk about their pictures with each other. Volunteers share their pictures in the circle.

Thinking about what they enjoy about themselves instead of 'Things I'm good at', for example, can result in very different insights for the children and for the facilitators. This is sometimes reflected in confidence groups as well, when children are encouraged to praise each other. For example, they might praise another child for something that they value in themselves.

EXPANSION ACTIVITY 8.2. SKILLS

Based on the discussion in 'Expansion activity 8.1. Three things I enjoy about myself', pairs of children draw a picture or write one thing they think their partner is skilled at and pin it on their partner's back. Each child tries to find out what their 'skill' is by walking around the room and asking other players questions, such as 'Is it to do with a sport?' or 'Is it to do with friends?'

EXPANSION ACTIVITY 8.3. LOADS OF AWARDS

For maximum effect I suggest that you also carry out 'Expansion activity 8.4. Things I'm working on either during the same session or at the next available opportunity – children are more likely to experience increased feelings of self-efficacy if they spend time talking about achievements with others.

For this activity each child thinks of five things that they have already achieved. They then imagine what it would be like to receive awards for these five things (see activity sheet 8.3). You could also set up a small award ceremony. Perhaps the children imagine that they are apprentice magicians or wellbeing experts. Use the 'scroll of honour' template (see Appendix C in *Using Imagination, Mindful Play and Creative Thinking to Support*

Wellbeing and Resilience in Children) for each child to write out their achievements. These can then be ceremoniously read out by a facilitator!

EXPANSION ACTIVITY 8.4. THINGS I'M WORKING ON

Emphasize to the children that these awards are for all the effort that is needed when we are working on something that we find difficult.

Children often think of these as 'Things I can't do' or 'Things I'm no good at'. Whenever appropriate, if you hear them using these phrases, you might suggest that they feel what it's like to change the words to 'I'm working on ____'. If it's something that they are not working on because they don't need to, then rather than 'I'm no good at this', they could try 'I don't need to learn/practise this' or 'I have chosen not to work on this'.

Talk about how it is okay to make mistakes when we are learning things. This is one way that we can discover how *not* to do things, and can sometimes help us to be more inventive in finding out successful ways to achieve our goals (see activity sheets 8.4a and 8.4b).

EXPANSION ACTIVITY 8.5. STAR TURN

Initiate a round of 'I'm brilliant at ____' in the group. Discuss the variety of things that come up. If you feel it's appropriate you could talk about how people get to be brilliant at something. For example, this might involve a discussion on learning sets of skills and building up ability gradually. This can be compared to having a natural ability at something that might nevertheless need to be practised and developed (such as singing).

Display pictures of 'Things I'm brilliant at'. See if the children can guess the owner of each picture.

55

9. Colourful me

Wellbeing focus:

☑ Self-confidence

Examples of personal skills learned or consolidated:

☑ Understanding metaphors ☑ Focusing attention

Examples of general/social learning:

☑ Building self-respect and respect for others

☑ Understanding and appreciating diversity

☑ Exploring self-concept

☑ Self-acceptance

Note: You will need to collect enough see-through plastic jars or bottles for each person to have their own (small plastic water bottles are ideal) and lots of different craft materials – the more varied the colours, the better.

There is no 'Talk about' section for this activity since there will be plenty of opportunity for spontaneous discussion during play.

How to play

Each child makes a container of talents and assets and things they like about themselves. They fill the container with layers of different materials or different colours of the same material, one layer to represent each talent (so layers may be of different thicknesses). It doesn't matter if some children end up shaking the container and mixing everything up. There will also be some 'settling' of materials, and some things will shift. Display the containers on shelves.

Adaptations

- Each child draws their own jar or bottle and colours in different shapes and layers inside to represent their talents, things that they enjoy doing, etc.
- The children make a container for things they appreciate about someone else and present it to them.

- The children draw a 'key' to what's in the jar or write an ingredients label.

EXPANSION ACTIVITY 9.1. THE STORIES WE TELL (2)

If you have not already done so, this would be an ideal time to introduce children to wellbeing stories. (See Chapter 17, 'Image-Making and Wellbeing Stories', and Chapter 18, 'Helping Children to Create Their Own Wellbeing Stories', in *Using Imagination, Mindful Play and Creative Thinking to Support Wellbeing and Resilience in Children*.)

You could perhaps tell a story that you have constructed specifically for this group or help the children to write or draw their own story based on the animal they chose in 'Expansion activity 6.4. If I were an animal' and some of the characteristics that they chose for '9. Colourful me'. Remind the children that their story will need to include a helper, a task to complete or a problem to solve, one or more obstacles to overcome and a positive resolution.

If appropriate, the children could work together in pairs or threes to construct their stories using each of their animal characters as protagonists or helpers.

IV

Phase Three: What Is Confidence?

AIMS

- To continue to strengthen group support and encourage supportive peer feedback.
- To explore self-confidence and what this means to individual children.
- To give the children opportunities to construct, lead and evaluate games.
- To introduce the children to stage 3 of the confidence groups.
- To strengthen the children's understanding of how feedback from others can help them to self-monitor.

SUGGESTED FORMAT AND NOTES

1. Pause to breathe.

2. General check-in.

3. Continue with praise and praise cards.

4. Choice of game from Phase Three.

5. Feedback/'Talk about'.

6. Second game or expansion activity.

7. Longer 'Talk about' and/or drawing time.

8. Confidence group stages 2 and 3/Closing activity: For confidence group stage 3, the children walk up to the speaker position, take time to settle themselves, look around the audience and then say one or two sentences appropriate to the theme for the day. After a brief silence, you could finish with each person having the chance to say one sentence beginning with 'I feel…', 'I noticed that…' or 'The story was…'

Once again, the other members of the group simply listen. The speaker is then given feedback by the facilitators and group members on particular skills, as appropriate. For example, the skill might be 'Acknowledging one of my successes to the whole group' and the speaker might say something like 'I swam two lengths of the swimming pool yesterday'. The children are not focusing on the achievement being acknowledged but instead are encouraged to give very specific feedback about what the speaker has just done, such as 'You smiled when you told us that, and you looked as though you felt really good about your success', 'You were very brave to go first and speak in front of the whole group', or 'You were great when you let Kirsty have a go before you'. Facilitators might include comments such as 'You looked so happy when you told us about your success. I felt really happy for you too'.

This sort of descriptive feedback will come from adult facilitators to start with in order to give an appropriate model, but children are usually quick to recognize all the different things they can praise in relation to confidence. The facilitators continue to praise group members for their positive feedback (for example, 'You picked up on a very important point in your feedback', 'You are really noticing how people show that they are feeling confident').

SUMMARY OF GAMES AND ACTIVITIES FOR PHASE THREE

10. **I can, you can**

    Expansion activities:

          10.1. Standing tall

          10.2. Change it

          10.3. Puzzles

          10.4. Confidence

    Theme: promoting feelings of self-efficacy

11. **Let's imagine**

    Expansion activity:

          11.1. I felt confident

    Themes: using imagery to help build self-confidence; further development of wellbeing stories

12. **Cinema sensation**

    Expansion activities:

          12.1. Confidence expert

          12.2. Images

          12.3. Try it out

    Themes: using imagery as an aid to setting goals; finding the 'inner expert', building competence and perceived self-efficacy

10. I can, you can

Wellbeing focus:

- ☑ Self-confidence

Examples of personal skills learned or consolidated:

- ☑ Taking turns
- ☑ Listening
- ☑ Observation

Examples of general/social learning:

- ☑ Building trust
- ☑ Appreciating diversity
- ☑ Development of body awareness and positive body image
- ☑ Developing flexibility of thought

This is a relatively brief game that can be played in preparation for children to engage with several expansion activities.

How to play

As a group, players think of a list of actions that everyone could do. The children volunteer to perform one of these for the rest of the group to copy. Each child who volunteers says 'My name is _____ and I can...hop, clap, stand on one leg', etc. The other players then all take one step forward, perform the action for 5 seconds, and then step back and wait for the next volunteer.

Adaptation

- The game coordinator plays music while the children do some exaggerated dance moves in a circle. Volunteers take one step forward and show a dance move for everyone else to copy.

Talk about

What does it feel like to move freely and not worry about 'getting it right'?

What does it feel like to have others try to follow your movement or dance?

EXPANSION ACTIVITY 10.1. STANDING TALL

In pairs the children alternate between a firm, stable posture and bowed head and hunched shoulders. Players sculpt each other until both agree that the feelings are different.

EXPANSION ACTIVITY 10.2. CHANGE IT

Invite ideas for a way to modify 'I can, you can' or to modify a game from the previous two phases.

In small groups of three or four the children try out their modified version and refine it if needed. They then demonstrate it to the rest of the group or lead the group in playing it.

Some children may be ready to invent a new game that could be used to demonstrate a particular set of skills, such as mending a bicycle puncture.

EXPANSION ACTIVITY 10.3. PUZZLES

The game coordinator teaches the group a magic trick or mind puzzle. Players are then asked to research another trick or puzzle to share with the group the next time that you meet.

It is worth building up a collection of magic tricks and mind puzzles for use in all groups, and they don't need to be very elaborate. Most of my favourites involve 'tricking' players into focusing on an unnecessary part of what I am doing. This can lead into useful discussions about focusing and attending. (See, for example, '4. The moon is round' in *Helping Children to Manage Friendships*, and for an exploration of focusing and attending, see Chapter 7, 'Helping Children to Be Mindful', in *Using Imagination, Mindful Play and Creative Thinking to Support Wellbeing and Resilience in Children*.) In relation to building confidence, children love to collect facts that no one else knows about, and tricks that 'astound' – a mini boost to their perceptions of self-efficacy.

An example of a quick mind puzzle is to ask someone to think of a three-digit number, reverse the number and take the lesser from the greater. Ask them to give you the first number of the answer. You will then be able to tell them the whole answer. How? The middle number will always be nine and the other two numbers will always add up to nine!

EXPANSION ACTIVITY 10.4. CONFIDENCE

In preparation for the next activity, the children complete activity sheet 10.4 and share their thoughts in the group if they want to.

11. Let's imagine

Wellbeing focus:

☑ Self-confidence

Examples of personal skills learned or consolidated:

☑ Listening
☑ Concentration

☑ Understanding opposites

Examples of general/social learning:

☑ Appreciating diversity
☑ Exploring self-concept

☑ Building self-respect and respect for others

Note: Remind children that all images should be accepted in a non-judgemental and respectful way.

Invite the children to settle themselves into a comfortable position in their chairs or sitting on the floor. Read the following activity slowly, with plenty of pauses to give them time to explore their images. Ask for feedback as appropriate: 'Would anyone like to tell us their image for confidence?' (For an example of encouraging feedback during imagery activities, see Chapter 9, 'Image-Making', in *Using Imagination, Mindful Play and Creative Thinking to Support Wellbeing and Resilience in Children*.)

Confidence

Close your eyes and take three full breaths to help you to feel relaxed. As you breathe out the first breath, relax your shoulders... As you breathe out the second breath, relax your arms... As you breathe out the third time, relax your fingers...

Ask your imagination to give you an image that somehow shows us what it's like to be confident. The image could be an animal, a plant or an object – anything at all. Just close your eyes and see what your imagination comes up with.

Can you picture it in your mind? What can you see? Have a good look at the image.

When you are ready imagine that you can become the image. Step into being the image of confidence... Take your time and really feel what this is like... What do you look like?... Do you move? How do you move?... Do you make a noise? What noises do you make?...

What do you think about?... What are the nice things about being this image of confidence?... Is there anything that is not so nice?...

Where do you live?... Who are your friends?... What do you do best?... What is the most important thing about you?...

If you could give some advice to children about being confident, what would you tell them?

When you have found out everything you can about being confident, come back to being you again... Thank your imagination for showing you this image... Let the image gradually fade away...

Remember that you can always call up the image again in the future if you want to remind yourself what it feels like to be as confident as this...

Come back to being in the room again...have a bit of a stretch and open your eyes.

When you are ready, draw or write about what it's like to be confident.

Talk about

How did the image of confidence move? What did it feel like to be so confident? Do you think it is possible to act in a confident way even when you are feeling a bit unsure? What do you think might happen if you did this?

What were the positive things about being this image? Was there anything that didn't feel comfortable or that felt unhelpful?

What is the opposite of feeling confident? Draw pictures to represent this opposite. Compare this with the confidence image and think about the differences.

The two images of confidence and its opposite can be used as the basis for a wellbeing story about how a protagonist builds their self-confidence. One possible way of doing this is described in Chapter 18 of *Using Imagination, Mindful Play and Creative Thinking to Support Wellbeing and Resilience in Children* (see 'Facilitating a story, version 1').

EXPANSION ACTIVITY 11.1. I FELT CONFIDENT

Using activity sheet 11.1, the children think of a time when they have already felt as confident as this.

Talk about

What was happening? How did you know that you felt confident? What could you feel in your body? What were you thinking about? How would other people have known that you felt confident?

12. Cinema sensation

Wellbeing focus:

☑ Self-confidence

Examples of personal skills learned or consolidated:

☑ Listening   ☑ Concentration
☑ Focusing attention

Examples of general/social learning:

☑ Building self-respect and respect   ☑ Exploring concepts of choice
   for others   and decision-making
☑ Exploring self-concept

This is an expanded version of a section of 'Spaceship to the stars', noted in Phase One as a useful imagery activity (see 'Expansion activity 4.2'). It is based on original ImageWork exercises by Dr Dina Glouberman.[1] Projecting yourself into the future to imagine how things will turn out is a powerful aid to making changes. Such imagery requires the suspending of judgement and reality in order to act 'as if' you had already achieved your desired outcome (see also 'Exploratory activity 1.3. Life paths' for facilitators).

The children start by thinking of a particular goal that they are working on. Alternatively, they can use this activity for an exploration of general self-confidence.

Read the following guidance slowly, with plenty of pauses, to allow time for the children to explore their imagery.

> Find a comfortable position...and gently let your eyes close. Take three full breaths, breathing in right down into the bottom of your lungs and breathing out slowly and calmly.
>
>   Let's imagine that you can go to your own private cinema. Imagine what that

---

1   See, for example, Glouberman, D. (2003) *Life Choices, Life Changes*. London: Hodder & Stoughton.

cinema looks like... If you go inside you will see a comfortable chair to sit in so that you can see the big cinema screen in front of you.

On to this screen walks a person...it's you! This is you after you've achieved your goal.

(If you are working with one child and you know what their goal is, it would be helpful to name it at this point.)

What do you look like on the screen?... What is the 'future you' doing now?... Now, let's imagine that you could walk right up to this cinema screen and step into being the future you. Imagine yourself doing just that. You get up out of your chair...you are walking towards the screen and now here you are – the future you. How does it feel to be you? How are you standing? How do you move? How is 'you' on the screen different from you sitting in the cinema?... What did you need to have, or to know, so that you could achieve your goal?... If the 'future you' could whisper something special to you in the cinema, what would they whisper?... How are you feeling now?

Time now to go back to being you sitting in the cinema. Imagine yourself stepping out of the screen and back to your seat. Ask yourself 'What did the future me whisper?' Notice if you feel any different now to how you felt when you first arrived at your cinema... When you are ready, imagine yourself walking away from the cinema. Feel yourself coming back to the room... Notice the feel of your body... Listen to the sounds around you... Keep your eyes closed for a little while longer while you have a little stretch... When you are ready open your eyes and look around you... Stamp your feet on the floor a bit to bring you properly back into the room!

EXPANSION ACTIVITY 12.1. CONFIDENCE EXPERT

(For a different way to 'meet the expert', see '6. Imagination tent' and '36. Inner expert' in *Helping Children to Manage Friendships*, another book in this series.)

Ask the children to think of someone who they all agree *appears* very confident. This might be a TV personality or a fictional character or someone they all know. Make a list together of all the things that this person does that causes them to appear confident. Be as specific as possible. If someone says 'They look confident', talk about how the person stands, walks, sits, dresses, their facial expression, etc. If they say 'They *sound* confident', talk about *how* they sound – Fast? Slow? Loud? Quiet? Somewhere in between?

When you have a comprehensive list reflecting the children's perceptions of a confident person, volunteers take turns to walk across the room, trying to keep this person in mind. They then sit in a designated chair (preferably not one that they usually use) and imagine themselves 'becoming' this person. They are now an expert in confidence and will be able to answer questions from the audience in a confident manner! It is best to have a set of questions prepared beforehand that will be easy to respond to, such as giving personal details, explaining how to give a dog a bath, or talking about their TV character.

Explore the idea that we all 'act' in different ways according to who we are with and according to the situation. Acting 'as if' we were someone else for a short period gives us the opportunity to explore how things would be if we chose to do things differently – it highlights that we have a choice in how we think and behave.

EXPANSION ACTIVITY 12.2. IMAGES

Imagine an image that represents 'confidence' and an image that represents 'bossy'. How are they different? How are they the same?

EXPANSION ACTIVITY 12.3. TRY IT OUT

Some children may be ready to facilitate a partner in 'finding an image' at this point. If you feel that this is appropriate, remind the group about what is acceptable in terms of feedback, discuss this brief five-step activity and trust them to have a go. Decide on what the image will represent (being relaxed, being 'cool', being brave) before the children take over the facilitation.

- Step 1: Breathe and relax.

- • Step 2: Invite an image to 'emerge'.
- • Step 3: Explore the image.
- • Step 4: Allow the image to fade.
- • Step 5: Come back to the room and shake your arms and hands or stamp your feet.

Phase Four: Making Changes, Facing Challenges

AIMS

- To further explore aspects of self-reliance.
- To help the children to extend their skills of active listening and giving and receiving supportive feedback.
- For children to experience increased confidence in speaking to the group and sharing knowledge and insights.
- To explore strategies for maintaining change.
- To review goals and plans for the future.

SUGGESTED FORMAT AND NOTES

1. Pause to breathe.

2. Brief check-in time.

3. Continue with praises and praise cards.

4. Play choice of Phase Four game.

5. Brief feedback/'Talk about'.

6. Second game or expansion activity.

7. Longer 'Talk about' and/or drawing time.

8. Confidence group stages 3 and 4/Closing activity: For confidence group stage 4, gradually increase the time for each person to speak when this feels right, but maximum time should be around three minutes. The content of this three-minute talk can now be more challenging and might include retelling a time of confidence and achievement, short stories about confidence or a performance poem. It might take the form of leading a game, explaining a magic trick or giving a summary of their understanding of self-confidence.

   Feedback at this stage is almost entirely from peers and from the speakers themselves: 'I used calm breathing before I started and I made sure that I took time to look at everyone', 'I felt calm and confident and that helped me to remember everything that I wanted to say'.

SUMMARY OF GAMES AND ACTIVITIES FOR PHASE FOUR

13. **Bravery awards**
    Expansion activities:
        13.1. I can change how confident I feel
        13.2. Film pitch
    Theme: promoting self-reliance

14. Obstacle course
    Expansion activity:
        14.1. Goals
    Themes: setting goals and monitoring progress

15. The stories we tell (3)
    Theme: story-telling as a way to embed feelings of self-efficacy

16. Just for fun
    Themes: preparing for the ending of a group; the importance of celebrations

13. Bravery awards

Wellbeing focus:

☑ Self-confidence

Example of personal skills learned or consolidated:

☑ Giving and receiving praise

Examples of general/social learning:

☑ Self-awareness
☑ Trust
☑ Taking turns

☑ Building self-respect and respect for others

How to play

Talk about times when we do something a *little bit* scary that might take some courage. Suggest very 'ordinary' situations (for example, first day at a new school, learning to ride a bike, diving into the pool for the first time, playing in the school concert). Encourage the children to think up at least 10 situations. Now think of ways in which we acknowledge someone else's bravery. This could be verbal praise, thumbs up, clapping, etc., or a full award ceremony. Do a round of 'I was brave when…' with each child choosing one situation from the list. The rest of the group acknowledge the child's bravery noisily and enthusiastically!

Adaptation

* Acknowledge small triumphs; times of making a 'wise decision'; times of solving a problem.

Talk about

Sometimes other people don't notice or don't know how we feel or what we've achieved. Just because they don't praise us doesn't mean that we didn't do well. It's important that we each learn to notice our own achievements and praise ourselves as well.

EXPANSION ACTIVITY 13.1. I CAN CHANGE HOW CONFIDENT I FEEL

The children spend time identifying some specific strategies that they will use to help them to continue to build and maintain their self-confidence (see activity sheet 13.1). The aim is also to help the children to see that the skills and qualities they already developed in other areas of life (such as perseverance and practice) can be very useful when they are setting their goals for building self-confidence (see Chapter 5, 'Making Experience Count', in *Using Imagination, Mindful Play and Creative Thinking to Support Wellbeing and Resilience in Children*).

Volunteers share their ideas with a partner or with the whole group. This could also be done in a confidence group activity.

A possible list might be:

I will reward myself when I have done well.

I will take care of myself by doing something relaxing every day.

I will answer at least one question in class every day.

I will learn to swim.

I will tell my teacher if I don't understand something.

I will talk to my mum about any worries I have.

I will make one new friend this term.

EXPANSION ACTIVITY 13.2. FILM PITCH

The children are given three different scenarios which involve a very specific challenge. These need to be within their personal sphere of experience or awareness. For example, being bullied, being lost or giving a presentation.

In pairs or groups of three the children choose one of these scenarios and construct a story board for a picture book or comic depicting a confident response to the challenge. Older children might enjoy constructing this with younger children in mind, to demonstrate an appropriate response.

The story board might include words and pictures drawn by the players or cut from a selection of magazines.

Once completed, the children decide how they will 'pitch' their idea to a publisher or to a producer who wants to make a film about confidence.

They then present their pitch in a confidence group or write a letter to the fictitious producer and read this to the group.

If possible, every child will need a photo or a copy of their story board and/or letter to add to their 'Book of Wisdom' if wanted.

14. Obstacle course

Wellbeing focus:

☑ Self-confidence

Examples of personal skills learned or consolidated:

☑ Cooperation   ☑ Problem-solving
☑ Negotiation

Examples of general/social learning:

☑ Thinking independently   ☑ Understanding the concept of
☑ Taking responsibility   inclusion
☑ Appreciating diversity

How to play

As a group, begin with a general discussion about obstacle courses. Have any of the children had experience of these? What sort of obstacles could you have? What safety issues might there be? How could organizers ensure that children of all ages and ability could join in?

Players work together in teams to design an obstacle course for a children's holiday activity. Overcoming each obstacle will require cooperation between potential players (see, for example, '23. Step up' in *Helping Children to Manage Transitions*, another title in this series). This can be done as a paper and pencil activity or as a model construction. Each team then shares their ideas with the whole group. The other players are encouraged to ask questions and request further explanations. They then give positive feedback to the presenting team.

Talk about

What happened in this activity? What worked? What didn't work?

Do we always have obstacles to overcome in order to achieve a goal?

Think of an obstacle that you have overcome. What helped you to overcome this? Did anyone else help you?

Of all the things that you have learned and achieved while playing these games, what skills and ideas will you use to help you to achieve your goals in the future?

EXPANSION ACTIVITY 14.1. GOALS

Use activity sheet 14.1 to prompt discussions about possible goals and how we might evaluate progress towards achieving that goal or modifying it in some way.

15. The stories we tell (3)

Make up wellbeing stories and/or puppet plays together using themes of:

- Working towards goals with a helper.
- 'Standing up' for something you believe in strongly.
- Coping with unexpected events.
- Standing up to peer pressure.

These stories can be very powerful learning experiences for children and are worth the investment of time and energy that they invariably involve. If possible, I suggest that you devote at least half the time spent in this phase to construct and rehearse a group play (or puppet play) to showcase the children's progress. Or, as an alternative, construct a group story and have every child take part in telling it.

16. Just for fun

Bringing a self-confidence group to a close requires some careful preparation. The children will have undoubtedly built a certain sense of security and safety within the group and will still be developing their confidence in other arenas. Inevitably, they will experience times when other children and adults are not so affirming or are not able to give supportive feedback in the same way that they have experienced in the confidence groups. They may need the chance to talk about their worries and future goals in some depth (see for example, 'Expansion activity 14.1. Goals') and perhaps to have the opportunity to arrange a follow-up session at some point in the near future. This can all take time but should not detract from the importance of the children also celebrating their achievements and noting how their growing resilience, determination and creativity will continue to help them to cope with future challenges.

'Just for fun' is therefore much more than the title suggests! This is a chance for children to choose a game that they have enjoyed and would like to play again before they leave the group. This gives them the opportunity to remind themselves that they can have fun while trying out different strategies and skills, and perhaps will also demonstrate how their confidence has grown since they first played the game.

After one or two games, I suggest completing the last confidence group activity with an award ceremony (perhaps a certificate for each child), generous applause and an informal group celebration with cake, fruit and general chat.

Activity Sheets

The activity sheets in this section can be adapted for discussion or used as a basis for devising more complex activity sheets for older children.

Where possible, I suggest that you encourage children to draw rather than to write, and to work together rather than to sit quietly completing activity sheets on their own. This sharing and talking will not only help to foster collaborative, mutually respectful relationships; it also offers an opportunity for each child to enrich their understanding of the benefits of using imagery, being mindful and thinking creatively.

The Book of Wisdom

THIS BOOK BELONGS TO

_____

ACTIVITY SHEET 1.2. NAME ASSOCIATIONS

Remembering other people's names is an important skill and there are lots of ways that you can help yourself to do this. One way is to think of the person's name together with something else – perhaps an object, something they like doing, or a colour that they like to wear. For each person in your group, write or draw something that will help you to remember their name.

Name of group member   My memory aid

ACTIVITY SHEET 4.1. WISDOM RULES!

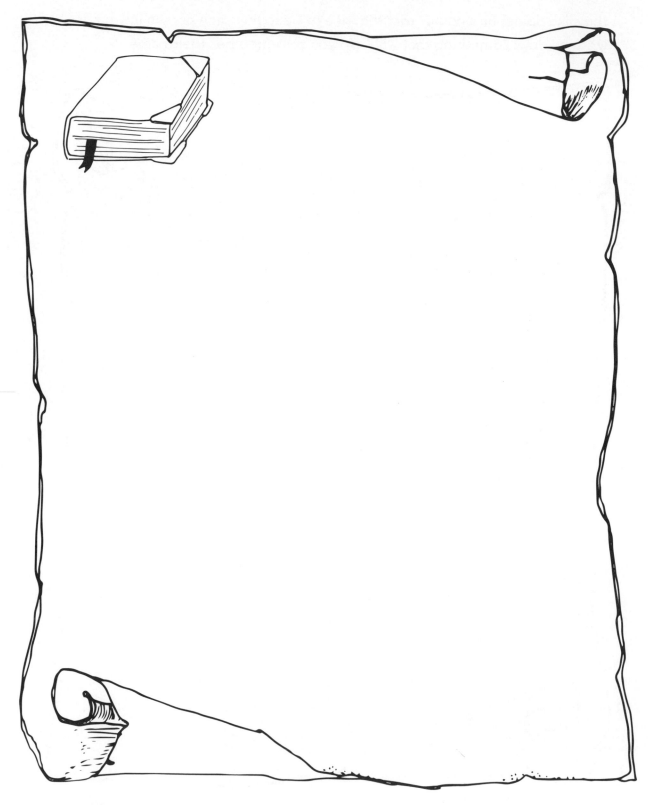

ACTIVITY SHEET 5.1. ACHIEVEMENTS

What does the word 'achievement' mean?

....

....

Can you think of one thing that you have achieved just a little while ago to write in the first star or planet?

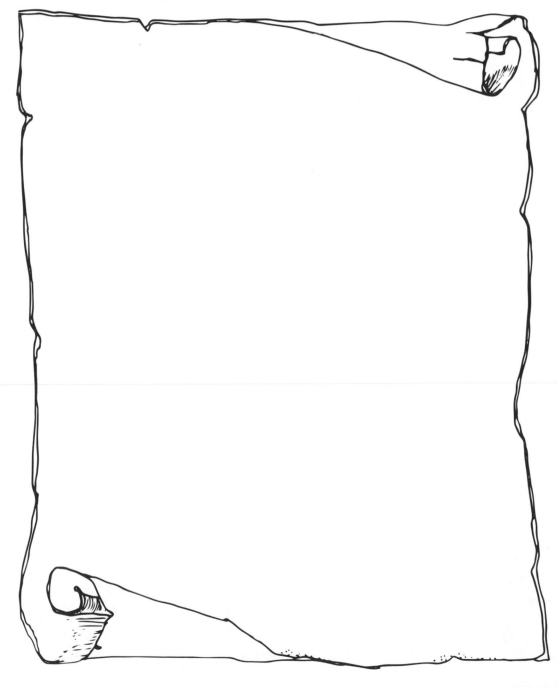

85

ACTIVITY SHEET 6.1. IS THIS ME?

Imagine that someone is writing about you for a newspaper. How would you like to be described?

ACTIVITY SHEET 6.3. PORTRAITS

ACTIVITY SHEET 8.3. LOADS OF AWARDS

Imagine that you have been invited to an award ceremony. You are going to be awarded for five achievements! Someone important calls out your name and reads out the list of your five achievements. Everyone claps as you go to receive your award. What do you get? How do you feel? Draw or write about your award ceremony.

ACTIVITY SHEET 8.4A. THINGS I'M WORKING ON

All through life we are learning new things and often getting better at some of the things we can already do or that we already know about. Let's imagine that you have been nominated to receive an award for the things that you are working on.

These are the things that you know are a bit difficult for you at the moment, so you are working on learning a bit more about them or practising regularly so they'll get easier for you.

Think of five things that you are working on and write them here.

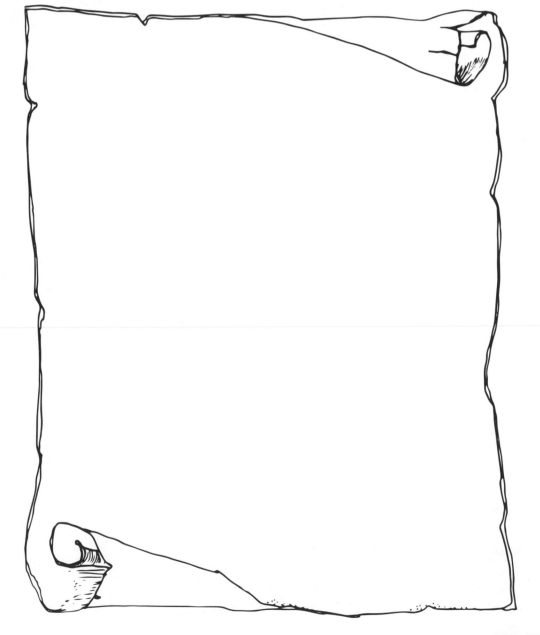

ACTIVITY SHEET 8.4B. MORE AWARDS

Imagine yourself at the award ceremony again. Your name is called and someone important reads out your list of the five things you are working on. Everyone claps and cheers as you go up to fetch your award. What do you get? How do you feel? Draw or write about it here.

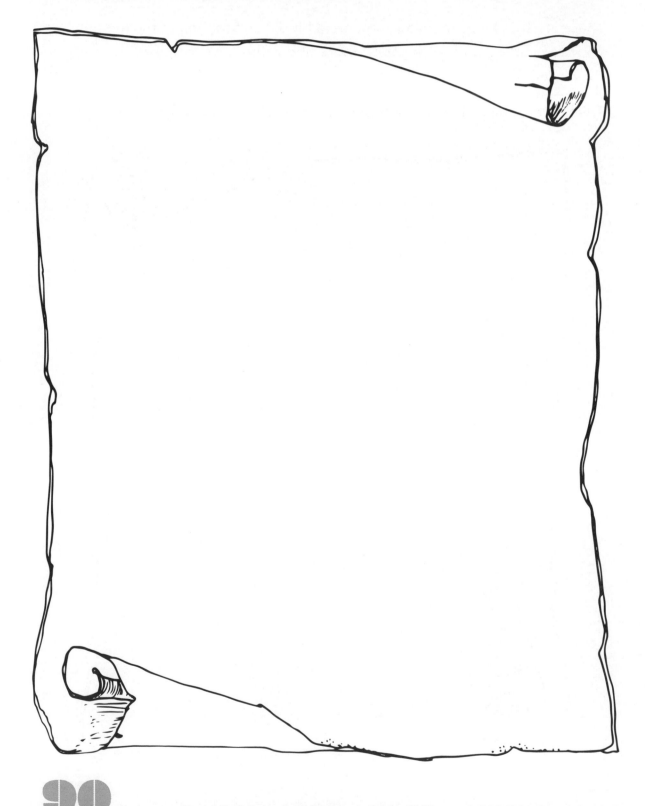

ACTIVITY SHEET 10.4. CONFIDENCE

What does the word 'confidence' mean?

....

....

Some people can seem to be very confident. Most of us are confident in some things we do and in some places. We have to build up our confidence with other things.

Think about one thing that you would like to be able to do with more confidence. Draw or write about it here.

ACTIVITY SHEET 11.1. I FELT CONFIDENT

Think of a time when you have felt confident. Draw or write about it here.

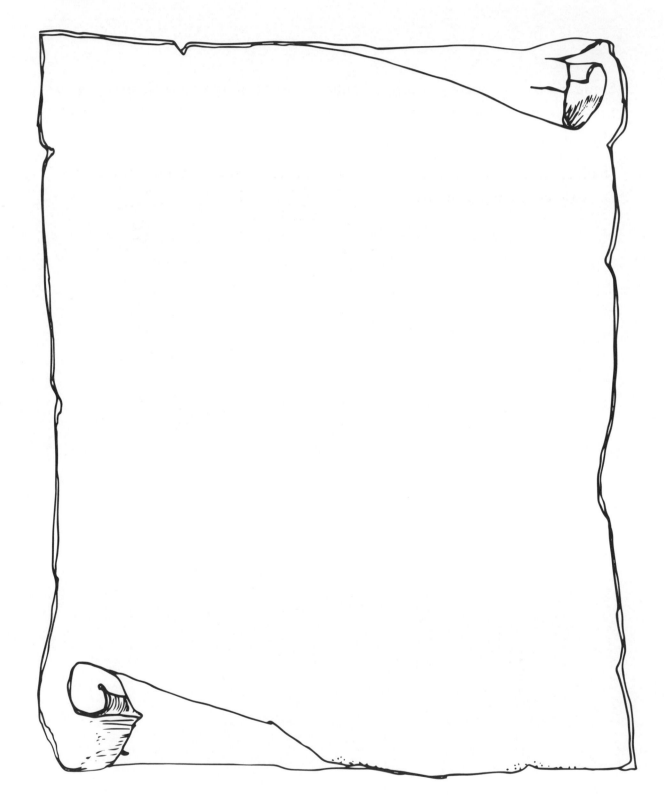

ACTIVITY SHEET 13.1. I CAN CHANGE
HOW CONFIDENT I FEEL

.... ☐

.... ☐

.... ☐

.... ☐

.... ☐

.... ☐

.... ☐

.... ☐

Put a tick in each box when you have tried your idea.

ACTIVITY SHEET 14.1. GOALS

Goal record sheet

My goal is:

....

....

....

....

I tried it when:

....

....

....

....

This is what happened:

....

....

....

....

The next thing I'm going to try is:

....

....

....

....